NATIONAL GEOGRAPHIC **OUR WORLD**

Stone Soup

A folk tale from France

Retold by Mary Quinn

NATIONAL
GEOGRAPHIC
L E A R N I N G

T0349764

This soldier is hungry. He hasn't got any food or any money. But he has got an idea.

2

The soldier puts some water and a stone in his pot.

The people ask, 'What are you doing?'

The soldier says, 'I'm making stone soup!'

The soldier tastes the soup.

'The soup is good,' he says.
'But it needs a carrot or two.'

4

The soldier asks a young woman, 'Have you got any carrots?'

The young woman gives him some carrots. He puts them in the pot.

The soldier tastes the soup.

'The soup is good,' he says.
'But it needs some beans.'

6

The soldier asks an old woman, 'Have you got any beans?'

The old woman gives him some beans. He puts them in the pot.

7

The soldier tastes the soup.

'The soup is good,' he says. 'But it needs some sweetcorn and a tomato or two.'

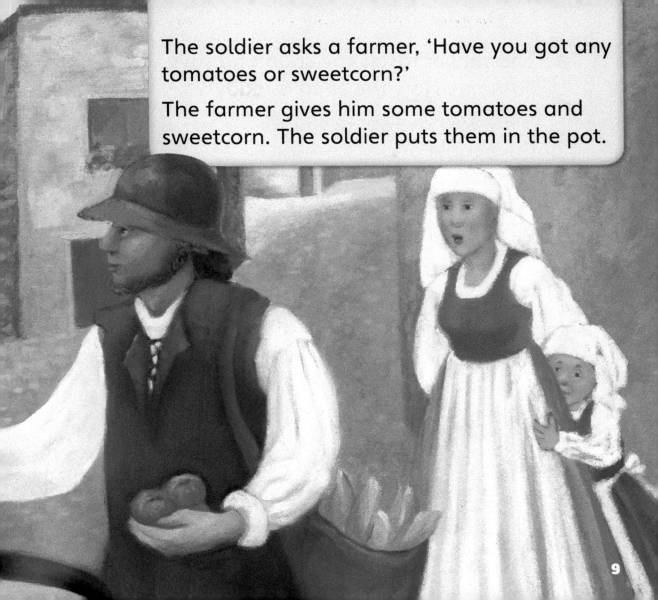

The soldier asks a farmer, 'Have you got any tomatoes or sweetcorn?'

The farmer gives him some tomatoes and sweetcorn. The soldier puts them in the pot.

9

The soldier tastes the soup and says, 'Mmmm. Now the soup is ready!'

'May we have some soup?' the people ask.

Facts About Food

Some foods grow under the ground. Carrots and potatoes grow under the ground.

carrots

potatoes

Some foods grow above the ground. Tomatoes and grapes grow above the ground.

tomatoes

grapes

Do you know any other foods that grow under or above the ground?

Fun with Food

Colour each food.
Then match the word to the food.

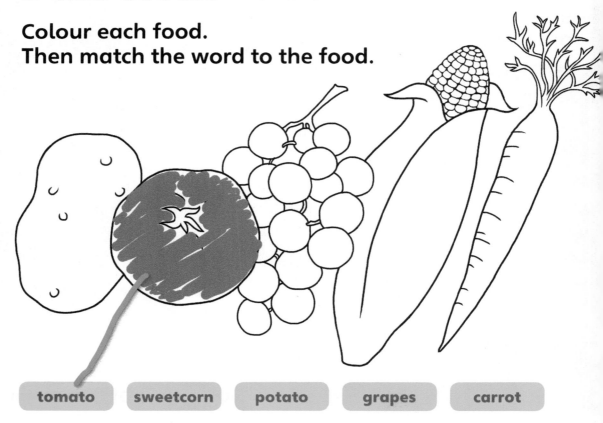

| tomato | sweetcorn | potato | grapes | carrot |

What foods can you see?
Write the name of each food.

carrot   beans   grapes
potato   tomato

grapes

Glossary

idea

money

pot

share

soldier

stone

taste